Nonelementary Integrals

Indefinite Nonintegrable Functions

Dharmendra Kumar Yadav

Assistant Professor of Mathematics

Lalit Narayan Mithila University

Darbhanga, Bihar

NOTION PRESS

Contents

Foreword

Nonelementary integral is a theory of non-antiderivative functions, where it is decided that whether an elementary function is indefinite integrable or not i.e., whether it has antiderivative or not. Traditionally it is known as nonelementary functions.

These types of functions are generally not discussed as a chapter in the Calculus book, although it has so many applications in Statistics, Physics, Engineering, etc. So it has relevance in Calculus and is useful for students of graduate, post graduate and research scholars as well.

In the present book, Dr. D. K. Yadav has presented the important theorems and properties of elementary and nonelementary functions with sufficient number of examples. He has also mentioned some old and his own six conjectures. So it will play a major role for research.

The writing of this book was a difficult task. Dr. Yadav deserves to be congratulated on his outstanding job for contributing so much to present the hidden properties of nonelementary functions of integration for mathematics readers. I wish him all the best for the book.

Prof. (Dr.) Kumari Priyanka

Department of Mathematics

Shivaji College, University of Delhi

New Delhi 110027

15.08.2023

Preface

Dr. D. K. Yadav completed his doctoral degree on such functions with the thesis entitled "A Study of Indefinite Nonintegrable Functions" from Vinoba Bhave University, Hazaribag, Jharkhand, under the supervision of Dr. Dipak Kumar Sen, Associate Professor of Mathematics, R. S. More College, Govindpur, Dhanbad.

We, Dr. Pankaj Kumar Manjhi, Assistant Professor; Dr. R. K. Dwivedi, Associate Professor & Head; Prof. D. S. Lal, Prof. A. B. Kumar, Prof. Arun Kumar, Prof. S. K. Agrawal, were the witness of his research work from the pre-registration test and seminar (March, 2008) to his viva-voce (December, 2013) of the Ph. D. degree.

During his research work, he called such integrals as indefinite nonintegrable functions in his all papers, thesis, documents, presentation and discussion. So undoubtably the book is a must read book for mathematics learners and more useful for mathematics teachers cum research scholars. For his great contributions I thank wish him all the best for his career.

Dr. Pankaj Kumar Manjhi

Assistant Professor of Mathematics

Vinoba Bhave University, Hazaribag, Jharkhand

Guide's Word

As per my memory Dr. D. K. Yadav had discussed such functions and Example 9.5 with me in 1995, when he was an under graduate first year student of Mathematics (Hons) in R. S. P. College, Jharia, Dhanbad, Bihar.

After seeing the present book and the materials discussed in it, I found that he has presented all those theorems and properties of Integral Calculus, which are generally not found in Calculus or Integral Calculus textbooks. It seems that he has poured all those methodologies of his doctoral research works in this book, which he had discussed earlier with me.

Dr. Peeyush Tewari, Director, Birla Institute of Technology, Jaipur Campus, Rajasthan was the external examiner in his Viva-Voce and he appreciated his work in the public. At that time he was working as an Associate Professor in Birla Institute of Technology, Noida Campus, Uttar Pradesh. His appreciation was also a symbol of good research and new concept of mathematical research in our university department.

With this book I am visiting again around his thesis and remembering the days of my supervision for his highest academic degree. So in my opinion the present book will be beneficial for all the mathematics learners, integration lovers and for those research scholars having interest in special type of integrals. Without studying the theorems and properties discussed in this book, no further research is possible. In fact this book is a research oriented book on Integral Calculus. I wish him all the best for his writing, teaching and research career.

Dr. Dipak Kumar Sen

Associate Professor (Retired)

R. S. More College, Govindpur, Dhanbad

Acknowledgments

Nonelementary integrals can also be called as indefinite nonintegrable functions because it indicates the exact meaning of the concerned functions in context of antiderivatives. I used this name in my all research papers and thesis work because at the time of submission of synopsis for Ph. D. degree, I was not ware of the classical name.

I am thankful to Prof. (Dr.) S. K. Agrawal, the then Dean of Science, Vinoba Bhave University, Hazaribag, who suggested me to do more research and review about my proposed research. Due to his lovely warning that 'he will not allow me to submit the thesis if I don't do some unique work and couldn't prove the proposed conjectures using proper properties' I could learn more about elementary and nonelementary functions. In fact his strict threaten provoked me for deep study.

As far as my journey of such functions is concerned, it started in 1995, when I was preparing for IITJEE in Patna. One classmate asked me to find the area surrounded by the boundries of three coins of radius 1 cm attached to each other. I replied it and then asked, can you find the following indefinite integral

$$\int \frac{e^{sinx}}{\cos x}\, dx \ ?$$

This suddenly came into my mind by taking some reverse case of the standard formula of integration:

$$\int e^{f(x)} f'(x)\, dx = e^{f(x)} + K$$

In this formula the derivative of f(x) is multiplied with $e^{f(x)}$ and I took its reverse and divided $e^{f(x)}$ by the derivative of f(x), which was a mid game of hardly five seconds. I with him found no solution. I then asked my favourite professor Dr. D. K. Sen (later he became my Ph. D. Supervisor in 2008) about it. He hinted to use partial fractions and I did that. Later I found, that solution was not true. Again I aksed Dr. Sen sir but he suggested me to do post graduate course first for it as I was in under graduate course at that time.

I continued to work on it and found **six standard forms of functions** which could not be integrated in 1995. I published these in a journal Acta Ciencia Indica Mathematics published by Pragati Prakashan, Meerut, Uttar Pradesh, India in 2007 with some errors because I was afraid and deliberately did some mistakes, so that if someone copies it, I shall claim my authorship on it with corrections.

But in 2008 I decided to persue Ph. D. on this and gave its revised forms with my supervisor Dr. D. K. Sen sir in the same journal.

Thus I started my doctoral research work in playing with friends and my best childhood friend Ramashish Prasad Saw 'Lal' always encouraged me for this. Then I tried to find its solution by introducing dominating sequential functions and completed my doctoral research work on it in 2012.

My thesis is available online and has been published by Grin Verlag Publishing, Germany in 2017. I also published two books on my doctoral research work entitled Six Conjectures on Integration and Dominating Sequential Functions by Grin Verlag Publishing.

I also thank my colleagues Prof. (Dr.) N. K. Agrawal; Dr. Ayaz Ahmad, Associate Professor and Head; Dr. S. N. Roy, Associate Professor; Dr. Abhimanyu Kumar, Assistant Professor; Dr. Vipul Snehi, Assistant Professor and Dr. Neha Varma, Assistant Professor, University Department of Mathematics, Lalit Narayan Mithila University for always encouraging me to write this book.

At the last but not the least, I would love to give my heartily thanks to my friends Dr. Dinesh Kumar Majhi, Dr. Awadh Kumar Yadav, Dr. Satyendra Kumar Satya, Dr. Deepti Lohia, Dr. Vandana Rajpal, Prof. (Dr.) Aparna Jain, Prof. (Dr.) Shivkumar Sahdev, Mr. Manish Kumar Meena, Mr. Jitendra Kumar Singh, Mr. Satish Kumar Hataria, Dr. Satish Kumar, etc. for their continuous encouragement.

Dr. Dharmendra Kumar Yadav

Why this Book?

Mathematics is not only a queen of all sciences but a miracle also. It needs not only talent to understand but seriousness cum care in applying the mathematical facts and formula. A little mistake changes the whole facts in seconds. So remembering formula and putting values is not mathematics but understanding their scope of applications is more important.

From school time we remember the formula in Trigonometry

$$\cos 2\theta = \frac{1 - \tan^2\theta}{1 + \tan^2\theta}$$

If we put $\theta = \frac{\pi}{2}$ in the above formula, we get

$$\cos 2\left(\frac{\pi}{2}\right) = \frac{1 - \tan^2\left(\frac{\pi}{2}\right)}{1 + \tan^2\left(\frac{\pi}{2}\right)}$$

$$\Rightarrow \cos(\pi) = \frac{1 - \tan^2\left(\frac{\pi}{2}\right)}{1 + \tan^2\left(\frac{\pi}{2}\right)}$$

$$\Rightarrow \cos(\pi) = \frac{1 - \infty}{1 + \infty}$$

$$\Rightarrow -1 = \frac{-\infty}{\infty} \Rightarrow \frac{\infty}{\infty} = 1$$

which is an absurd result. So what went wrong in the above calculation? We missed the concept of domain. The above formula is not valid for odd multiple of $\frac{\pi}{2}$.

The same care and seriousness is needed in integration. There is a well known technique of 'method of substitution' in integration, which is needed when the 'integrand' is not in the standard form, for which a readymade formula of integration is available. To understand it let us find the value of the definite integral

$$\int_{-1}^{1} \frac{dx}{1 + x^2}$$

We know that

$$\int_{-1}^{1} \frac{dx}{1 + x^2} = [\tan^{-1} x]_{-1}^{1}$$

$$= \tan^{-1}(1) - \tan^{-1}(-1)$$

$$= \frac{\pi}{4} + \frac{\pi}{4} = \frac{\pi}{2}$$

Now putting $x = \frac{1}{z}$ in the integrand and accordingly changing the limits, we see that

$$\int_{-1}^{1} \frac{dx}{1 + x^2} = -\int_{-1}^{1} \frac{dz}{1 + z^2}$$

$$= -[\tan^{-1} z]_{-1}^{1}$$

$$= -\tan^{-1}(1) + \tan^{-1}(-1)$$

$$= -\frac{\pi}{4} - \frac{\pi}{4} = -\frac{\pi}{2}$$

Both results are different. So not every substitution is suitable for changing the variable in an integrand and care must be taken while applying it.

So in studying mathematics special care is needed. This book is an attempt in Integral Calculus specially in finding the antiderivative of elementary functions, whose integral is not an elementary function. Many important theorems and properties have been discussed, which are generally not discussed in Calculus and Integral Calculus textbooks.

During my doctoral research work I got aware about such concepts of nonelementary functions. I didn't find all these concepts in a single book or research article but collected from many research papers, thesis and books. At the final submission of my thesis I dreamt to publish a book on indefinite nonintegrable functions for the benefit of integration and mathematics lovers. The present book is the output of that dream.

Dr. Dharmendra Kumar Yadav

1. Introduction

The problem considered in the book is generally known as the problem of 'indefinite integration or antiderivative' i.e., the problem 'to find a function whose differential coefficient is a given function'.

To make it clear let us consider a real valued continuous function $f(x)$ of the real variable x and we want to determine a function $F(x)$, whose differential coefficient is $f(x)$. In other words, we want to solve the differential equation

$$\frac{dF(x)}{dx} = f(x) \qquad (1.1)$$

For the above differential equation (1.1) following questions may arise:

Case-I: Does the function $F(x)$ always exist?

Case-II: Has the differential equation (1.1) always a solution?

Case-III: Is the solution, if it exists, unique?

Case-IV: What will be the relation among different solutions, if it has more than one solution?

Case-V: What will happen if such $F(x)$ doesn't exist?

The answers of these questions are contained in 'definite integral'. Here the definite integral

$$F(x) = \int_a^x f(t)dt \qquad (1.2)$$

is a solution of the differential equation (1.1), which is also defined as the 'limit of a certain sum'.

Further $F(x) + C$ is also a solution of the differential equation (1.1), where C is an arbitrary constant. All other solutions of the differential equation (1.1) will be of the form $F(x) + C$.

Sometimes we say that the problem of indefinite integration is that of 'finding an expression for $F(x)$, when $f(x)$ is given'. The theory of definite integrals provides the solution with an expression in the form of a limit.

But the problem of indefinite integration as discussed above lacks in precision. This problem can be stated precisely only when we introduce the restrictions to the 'class of functions' and the 'modes of expression' which we are taking into consideration in the book.

Another solution of differential equation (1.1) is given by integrating both sides as follow

$$\int dF(x) = \int f(x)\, dx$$

$$\Rightarrow F(x) = \int f(x)\, dx + K$$

Now the problem is

$$\int f(x)\, dx\, ?$$

Can we find it for all elementary functions $f(x)$? The prime goal of this book is to answer this question and present the developed theorems and properties related to this problem.

Solved Examples

Example-1.1: Solve the differential equation

$$\frac{dF(x)}{dx} = x^2 + x.$$

Solution: We have

$$\frac{dF(x)}{dx} = x^2 + x$$

Integrating both sides, we get

$$\int dF(x) = \int (x^2 + x)\, dx$$

$$\Rightarrow F(x) = \frac{x^3}{3} + \frac{x^2}{2} + K$$

So

$$F(x) = \frac{x^3}{3} + \frac{x^2}{2} + K$$

is the function, which when differentiated gives us

$$f(x) = x^2 + x$$

as can be seen below

$$\frac{dF(x)}{dx} = \frac{d}{dx}\left(\frac{x^3}{3} + \frac{x^2}{2} + K\right)$$

$$= \frac{3.x^2}{3} + \frac{2.x}{2} + 0 = x^2 + x$$

Thus we see the close relationship between differentiation and indefinite integration (or antidifferentiation).

Example-1.2: Solve the differential equation

$$\frac{dF(x)}{dx} = \frac{\sin x}{x}.$$

Solution: We have

$$\frac{dF(x)}{dx} = \frac{\sin x}{x}$$

Integrating both sides, we get

$$\int dF(x) = \int \frac{\sin x}{x}\, dx$$

$$\Rightarrow F(x) = \int \frac{\sin x}{x}\, dx$$

We cannot find it in compact form. But using equation (1.2), the definite integral concept, we can write it as

$$F(x) = \int \frac{\sin x}{x}\, dx = \int_{a}^{x} \frac{\sin t}{t}\, dt$$

After giving some values to a and x, we can find it is terms of limit of a sum i.e., in a series. Because there does not exist any elementary function f(x), which when differentiated gives $\frac{\sin x}{x}$.

Exercise-1

1. Derive a relation between indefinite integration and a differential equation.

2. Derive a relation between definite integration and a differential equation.

3. Derive a relation between indefinite integration and a definite integration.

4. Solve the following differential equations:

    a. $\dfrac{dF(x)}{dx} = \dfrac{e^x}{x}$

    b. $\dfrac{dF(x)}{dx} = e^x + x$

    c. $\dfrac{dF(x)}{dx} = e^x + \sin x$

    d. $\dfrac{dF(x)}{dx} = e^{x^2} + x$

    e. $\dfrac{dF(x)}{dx} = \sin x + x$

    f. $\dfrac{dF(x)}{dx} = \sin x + \log x$

2. Limit in Antiderivative

We know that if $y = f(x)$ is an elementary function then its differential coefficient is also an elementary function and is denoted and defined by

$$\frac{dy}{dx} = \frac{df(x)}{dx} = \lim_{\Delta x \to 0} \frac{f(x + \Delta x) - f(x)}{\Delta x}$$

provided that the limit exists finitely. Integrating both sides, we get

$$\int df(x) = \int \lim_{\Delta x \to 0} \frac{f(x + \Delta x) - f(x)}{\Delta x} dx$$

$$\Rightarrow f(x) = \int \lim_{\Delta x \to 0} \frac{f(x + \Delta x) - f(x)}{\Delta x} dx \qquad (2.1)$$

which can also be written as

$$\Rightarrow f(x) = \lim_{\Delta x \to 0} \int \frac{f(x + \Delta x) - f(x)}{\Delta x} dx \qquad (2.2)$$

Both equations (2.1) and (2.2) are equal. Expresssion (2.1) can be proved as

$$f(x) = \int \lim_{\Delta x \to 0} \frac{f(x + \Delta x) - f(x)}{\Delta x} dx$$

$$= \int \frac{df(x)}{dx} dx = \int df(x) = f(x)$$

Thus we get the well known relation between differentiation and antidifferentiation

$$f(x) = \int \frac{df(x)}{dx}\, dx$$

Solved Examples

Example-2.1: Examine the property (2.1) and (2.2) for the elementary function $f(x) = \sin x$.

Solution: From property (2.1), we have

$$\int df(x) = \int \lim_{\Delta x \to 0} \frac{f(x + \Delta x) - f(x)}{\Delta x}\, dx$$

Putting $f(x) = \sin x$, we get

$$\int d\sin x = \int \lim_{\Delta x \to 0} \frac{\sin(x + \Delta x) - \sin(x)}{\Delta x}\, dx$$

which implies that

$$\sin x = \int \lim_{\Delta x \to 0} \frac{2\cos\left(\frac{2x + \Delta x}{2}\right)\cdot \sin\left(\frac{\Delta x}{2}\right)}{\Delta x}\, dx$$

$$= \int \lim_{\Delta x \to 0} \cos\left(\frac{2x + \Delta x}{2}\right)\cdot \frac{\sin\left(\frac{\Delta x}{2}\right)}{\frac{\Delta x}{2}}\, dx$$

$$= \int \cos(x)\, dx = \int d(\sin x) = \sin x$$

Similarly by applying property (2.2), we have

$$\int df(x) = \lim_{\Delta x \to 0} \int \frac{f(x + \Delta x) - f(x)}{\Delta x}\, dx$$

Putting $f(x) = \sin x$, we get

$$\int d\sin x = \lim_{\Delta x \to 0} \int \frac{\sin(x + \Delta x) - \sin(x)}{\Delta x} dx$$

which implies that

$$\sin x = \lim_{\Delta x \to 0} \int \frac{2\cos\left(\frac{2x + \Delta x}{2}\right).\sin\left(\frac{\Delta x}{2}\right)}{\Delta x} dx$$

$$= \lim_{\Delta x \to 0} \frac{\sin\left(\frac{\Delta x}{2}\right)}{\frac{\Delta x}{2}} . \int \cos\left(\frac{2x + \Delta x}{2}\right) dx$$

$$= \lim_{\Delta x \to 0} \frac{\sin\left(\frac{\Delta x}{2}\right)}{\frac{\Delta x}{2}} . \frac{\sin\left(\frac{2x + \Delta x}{2}\right)}{\frac{2}{2}} = \sin x$$

Example-2.2: Examine the property (2.1) and (2.2) for the elementary function

$$f(x) = \frac{\sin x}{x}.$$

Solution: Since both properties are equal, we apply property (2.1) only.

We have

$$\int df(x) = \int \lim_{\Delta x \to 0} \frac{f(x + \Delta x) - f(x)}{\Delta x} dx$$

Putting $f(x) = \frac{\sin x}{x}$, we get

$$\int d\frac{\sin x}{x} = \int \lim_{\Delta x \to 0} \frac{\frac{\sin(x + \Delta x)}{x + \Delta x} - \frac{\sin x}{x}}{\Delta x} dx$$

which implies that

$$f(x) = \int \lim_{\Delta x \to 0} \frac{x.\sin(x + \Delta x) - (x + \Delta x).\sin x}{(x + \Delta x).x.\Delta x} dx$$

$$= \int \lim_{\Delta x \to 0} \frac{x.\{\sin(x + \Delta x) - \sin x\} - \Delta x.\sin x}{(x + \Delta x).x.\Delta x} dx$$

$$= \int \lim_{\Delta x \to 0} \frac{x.2\cos\left(\frac{2x + \Delta x}{2}\right).\sin\left(\frac{\Delta x}{2}\right) - \Delta x.\sin x}{(x + \Delta x).x.\Delta x} dx$$

Let us first find the limit under the integral sign i.e.,

$$\lim_{\Delta x \to 0} \frac{x.2\cos\left(\frac{2x + \Delta x}{2}\right).\sin\left(\frac{\Delta x}{2}\right) - \Delta x.\sin x}{(x + \Delta x).x.\Delta x}$$

$$= \lim_{\Delta x \to 0} \left\{ \frac{x.2\cos\left(\frac{2x + \Delta x}{2}\right).\sin\left(\frac{\Delta x}{2}\right)}{(x + \Delta x).x.\Delta x} - \frac{\Delta x.\sin x}{(x + \Delta x).x.\Delta x} \right\}$$

$$= \lim_{\Delta x \to 0} \left\{ \frac{2\cos\left(\frac{2x + \Delta x}{2}\right).\sin\left(\frac{\Delta x}{2}\right)}{(x + \Delta x).\Delta x} - \frac{\sin x}{(x + \Delta x).x} \right\}$$

$$= \lim_{\Delta x \to 0} \left\{ \frac{\cos\left(\frac{2x + \Delta x}{2}\right)}{(x + \Delta x)} \frac{\sin\left(\frac{\Delta x}{2}\right)}{\frac{\Delta x}{2}} - \frac{\sin x}{(x + \Delta x).x} \right\}$$

$$= \left\{ \frac{\cos\left(\frac{2x + 0}{2}\right)}{(x + 0)}.1 - \frac{\sin x}{(x + 0).x} \right\}$$

$$= \left(\frac{\cos x}{x} - \frac{\sin x}{x^2} \right)$$

Therefore we have

$$f(x) = \int \left(\frac{\cos x}{x} - \frac{\sin x}{x^2} \right) dx$$

Putting the value of f(x), we get

$$\frac{\sin x}{x} = \int \left(\frac{\cos x}{x} - \frac{\sin x}{x^2} \right) dx$$

$$= \int d\left(\frac{\sin x}{x} \right)$$

$$= \frac{\sin x}{x}$$

Exercise-2

Verify the properties (2.1) and (2.2) for the following elementary functions:

(a) $f(x) = \dfrac{e^x}{x}$

(b) $f(x) = e^x + x$

(c) $f(x) = e^x + \sin x$

(d) $f(x) = e^{x^2} + x$

(e) $f(x) = \sin x + x$

(f) $f(x) = \sin x + \log x$

3. Elementary Functions

To understand nonelementary integrals we need to know the concepts of elementary functions. The concept of these functions is more useful than functions as far as the nonelementary or indefinite nonintegrable or non-antiderivative functions are concerned.

Function: Let us suppose that A and B are two non-empty sets, then a rule f(x) which associates each element x of A with a unique element y of B is called a mapping or function from A to B.

If f(x) is a function from A to B, we denote it by $f: A \rightarrow B$ and read it as f(x) is a function from A to B. If f(x) relates x of A to y of B, then we say that y is the image of the element x under the function f and denote it by y = f(x).

The set A is called the domain of the function and the set of all images of f(x) is called the range of the function. If the domain and range of the function f(x) are subsets of the set of real numbers R, then the function f(x) is said to be a real valued function.

Example 3.1: $f(x) = x^2$ is a real valued function from the set of natural numbers N to N.

Elementary Functions: We call a function an elementary function if it can be expressed as an equation in the form y = f(x), where f(x) represents an expression formed by the combination of a finite collection of powers of x, trigonometric functions, inverse trigonometric functions, hyperbolic functions, inverse hyperbolic functions, exponentials, and logarithms together through additions, subtractions, multiplications, divisions, powers, and compositions.

Example 3.2: Following functions

$$f(x) = \sin x + x$$

$$g(x) = 5x^2 + 2x - e^x$$

$$h(x) = \tanh x$$

$$i(x) = \log x$$

are elementary functions.

All functions are not elementary function. A function which is not elementary is known as a nonelementary function. A popular example of a nonelementary function is a piecewise defined function

$$f(x) = \begin{cases} 0, & \text{if x is rational} \\ 1, & \text{if x is irrational} \end{cases}$$

on [0, 1]. The function f(x) = [x] is also a nonelementary function. Many types of nonelementary functions arise in Integral Calculus as "anti-derivatives or indefinite integration" of elementary functions.

Exercise-3

Which of the following functions are elementary?

1. $f(x) = \sin x + |x|$

2. $g(x) = e^x + \log x$

3. $h(x) = x + [x]$

4. $i(x) = 4 + |x|$

5. $d(x) = 1 + x + \dfrac{x^2}{2} + \dfrac{x^3}{3} + \cdots$

6. $b(x) = \begin{cases} x + 4, & \text{if } x < 0 \\ 2, & \text{if } x = 0 \\ x - 5, & \text{if } x > 0 \end{cases}$

4. Antiderivative

Antiderivative (also known as indefinite integral) begins with a very simple definition as the 'reverse process of differentiation'. It has the origin in the process of summation and the words 'to integrate' literary means 'to find the sum of'. Later it was seen that integration can also be viewed as the 'reverse process of differentiation'.

The study of Integral Calculus consists of developing techniques for the determination of integral of a given function (in fact of elementary function).

Many pioneers of mathematicians has contributed in the development of the subject Calculus, but a large part of the subject was developed by Sir Isaac Newton (1642-1727) as a tool to help him to solve problems arose in connection with his investigations in Physics and Astronomy. But the credit for the invention of this subject must also be shared with a great mathematician G. W. Leibnitz (1646-1716), who independently, approximately and concurrently also developed a large part of the subject and whose notations almost universally has been adopted in preference to that used by Newton.

Integration: It is divided into two parts: indefinite and definite. The antiderivative (indefinite integral) is defined as the reverse process of differentiation. In other words, if f(x) is the differential coefficient of F(x), then antiderivative of f(x) is taken as F(x). Generally we write antiderivative of f(x) as F(x) + k, where k denotes an arbitrary constant and is called constant of integration. This F(x) + k is known as antiderivative of f(x) with respect to x. Therefore if

$$\frac{d}{dx}F(x) = f(x)$$

then the antiderivative of f(x) is denoted and defined by

$$\int f(x)dx = F(x) + k$$

The letter x in dx means that the antiderivative is to be performed with respect to the variable x. Here F(x) is called an integral of f(x) and F(x) + k is called the General Integral. The function which is to be integrated (antidifferentiated) is known as 'integrand'. The process of finding antiderivative is called antidifferentiation or integration and $\int f(x)dx$ is called an indefinite integral of f(x) with respect to x.

Any two indefinite integrals of the same elementary function differ by a constant. It may happen that by different methods of antiderivative, we get different indefinite integrals of the same elementary function, but it will always be seen that they differ from each other merely by a constant.

General Method: To find the antiderivative of an elementary function f(x), we try to find out an elementary function F(x) such that which when differentiated gives f(x).

For example, to find the antiderivative

$$\int \sin x \, dx$$

we know that when $-\cos x + k$ is differentiated, it gives $\sin x$. Therefore we have the indefinite integral

$$\int \sin x \, dx = -\cos x + k$$

But it must not be thought that every elementary function has got an antiderivative.

For example, the elementary functions

$$\frac{\sin x}{x}, e^{x^2}, \frac{\cos x}{x}, \frac{e^x}{x}$$

etc. are such functions, which has got no indefinite integrals, because there are not elementary functions which when differentiated gives us

$$\frac{\sin x}{x}, e^{x^2}, \frac{\cos x}{x}, \frac{e^x}{x}.$$

The antiderivatives of such functions have been called nonelementary functions or nonelementary integrals or indefinite nonintegrable functions in the book.

Note: Leibniz (1684) defined an antiderivative of an elementary function f(x) as a solution F(x) composed of elementary functions such that

$$\frac{d}{dx}F(x) = f(x)$$

As has been discussed in Chapter-1 that in mathematical symbol, it is also denoted by

$$F(x) = \int_{a}^{x} f(t)\, dt = \int f(x)\, dx + k$$

which on differentiation gives us $F'(x) = f(x)$, where the constant of integration k corresponds to the value of the indefinite integral for the lower limit a.

Example-4

Find the antiderivative of the following functions:

1. $f(x) = \frac{1}{x}$

2. $f(x) = \frac{1}{x^2}$

3. $f(x) = \sec x . \tan x$

4. $f(x) = \csc^2 x$

5. $f(x) = \frac{1}{(x+1)(x+2)}$

6. $f(x) = \frac{x^{n+1}}{n+1}, n \neq -1$

5. Nonelementary Integrals

The burning problem of this chapter and the book is that if the 'integrand' is an elementary function, is it necessary that the antiderivative is also an elementary function (if it exists) and if it is not so, then why?

Problem of Antiderivative: Let us consider that f(x) belongs to some class of functions S. Then we may ask whether F(x) (the antiderivative of f(x)) is a member of S, or can be expressed, according to some standard mode of expression, in terms of functions, which are members of S.

The extent of the problem depends upon the choice of:

(i) a class of functions, and

(ii) a standard mode of expression.

We take S as the class of *elementary functions*, and the mode of expression is taken as the *explicit expression in finite terms* i.e., in closed form.

Those functions whose indefinite integrals are neither elementary nor can be expressed in terms of elementary functions are classically known as *nonelementary functions*. These functions can also be named as *indefinite nonintegrable or simply nonintegrable or non-antiderivable functions*. In the present book, we have called them nonelementary integrals.

For example, the following functions

$$\frac{\sin x}{x}, e^{x^2}, \frac{e^x}{x}$$

are elementary functions, where as their antiderivative or indefinite integral

$$\int \frac{\sin x}{x}\,dx, \int e^{x^2}\,dx, \int \frac{e^x}{x}\,dx$$

are nonelementary integrals.

In other words, if we say that an indefinite integral of

$$\int f(x)dx$$

is elementary, it means that its integral exists and can be expressed in terms of elementary functions in closed form.

Lack of Notations of Functions: We know that the indefinite integral of an elementary function is the assertion of the well known theorem: Fundamental Theorem of Calculus: *Every continuous function has an antiderivative.* But it cannot be guaranteed that we can find a formula for an antiderivative in terms of elementary functions like sine, cosine, logarithm, and so forth.

There are elementary functions which have anti-derivatives but they cannot be expressed in terms of elementary functions due to the lack of notations of those functions.

For example:

$$\int e^{-x^2}\, dx, \ \int \frac{e^x}{x}\, dx, \ \int \frac{sinx}{x}\, dx, \ \int \frac{cosx}{x}\, dx$$

etc. are such indefinite integrals.

Note: By certain changes of variable we can get other nonelementary integrals from previous nonelementary integrals.

For example, the following indefinite integrals

$$\int e^{x^2}\, dx, \ \int \frac{e^x}{x}\, dx$$

are not elementary.

If we replace x by e^z in the second integral, we get

$$\int e^{e^z}\, dx$$

a nonelementary integral, and replacing x by logz, we get

$$\int \frac{dz}{logz}$$

a nonelementary integral.

The integral

$$\int log(logx)\, dx$$

reduces to the previous integral using integration by parts, so it also is nonelementary.

Therefore there is an obvious question arise in mind that how can we decide that which elementary function has got an indefinite integral and which one has not. Many efforts have been done to find the algorithm for elementary and nonelementary integrals of elementary functions. In the present book some of them have been discussed in next chapters onwards.

Exercise-5

Using the nonelementary integrals in this chapter, verify which of the following integrals is (are) nonelementary?

1. $\int e^{x^2}\, dx$

2. $\int \dfrac{e^{-x}}{x}\, dx$

3. $\int \dfrac{x}{sinx}\, dx$

4. $\int \ln\,[\ln\,\{\ln\,(x)\}]\, dx$

Well Known Nonelementary Integrals: We know that the process of integration generates new functions. Following are the list of new functions originated from nonelementary integrals:

Plasma Dispersion Function: It was propounded by *Fried* and *Conte* in **1961,** which is also known by **Fried-Conte function** is denoted and given by

$$Z(x) = \frac{1}{\sqrt{\pi}} \int_{-\infty}^{\infty} \frac{e^{-t^2} dt}{t - x}$$

Jackson Function: It was propounded by *Jackson* in **1960** and but it does not (yet) have accepted name (to the knowledge of Lehtinen, 2010) is given by

$$G(x) = \frac{1}{\sqrt{\pi}} \int_{-\infty}^{\infty} \frac{te^{-t^2} dt}{t - x}$$

Dawson Integral: It was presented by *Abramowitz* and *Stegun* in **1965**, which is sometimes called Dawson's function is given by

$$F(x) = e^{-x^2} \int_{0}^{x} e^{y^2} dy$$

Frensel Functions: It was introduced by *Abramowitz* and *Stegun* in **1965** and is denoted and defined by

$$C(x) + iS(x) = \int_0^x e^{i\pi t^2/2} \, dt$$

Fresnel Integrals: They are alternatively denoted and defined by

$$x(t) = \int_0^t \cos(x^2) \, dx$$

$$y(t) = \int_0^t \sin(x^2) \, dx$$

Sitenko Function: It was given by *Sitenko* in **1982** and is defined by

$$\varphi(x) = 2x e^{-x^2} \int_0^x e^{t^2} \, dt$$

Function Y(x): It is due to *Fried* and *Conte* given in **1961** and is defined by

$$Y(x) = \frac{e^{-x^2}}{x} \int_0^x e^{t^2} \, dt$$

Gordeyev Integral: It was propounded by *Gordeyev* in **1952** and is defined by

$$G_v(w, \lambda) = w \int_0^\infty e^{\left[iwt - \lambda(1 - \cos t) - \frac{vt^2}{2} \right]} dt$$

Error or **Cramp Function:** It was introduced by *Gauss*. Some Russian authors Mikhailovskiy (1975), Bogdanov et al. (1976) call erf(x) a **Cramp function**. It is given by

$$erf(x) = \frac{2}{\sqrt{\pi}} \int e^{-x^2} dx$$

$$\text{or, } erf(z) = \frac{2}{\sqrt{\pi}} \int_0^z e^{-t^2} dt$$

Complementary Error Function: It is given by

$$erfc(x) = \frac{2}{\sqrt{\pi}} \int_x^\infty e^{-t^2} dt = 1 - erf(x)$$

Exponential Integral: It is denoted and defined by

$$Ei(x) = \int \frac{e^x}{x} dx$$

Sine and Cosine Integrals: They are defined by

$$Si(x) = \int \frac{\sin x}{x} dx$$

$$Ci(x) = \int \frac{\cos x}{x} dx$$

Logarithmic Integral: It is denoted and defined by

$$\mathrm{li}(x) = \int_0^x \frac{1}{\log t}\, dt$$

$$\text{or, } \mathrm{li}(x) = \int \frac{dx}{\log x}$$

Faddeeva Function: It was introduced by *Fadeeva* and *Terent'ev* in **1954**. It is also called *complex error function* or *probability integral* by Weideman (1994), Baumjohann and Treumann (1997). Some Russian authors Mikhailovskiy (1975), Bogdanov et al. (1976) call it *Complex Cramp function.* It is given by

$$w(x) = e^{-x^2}\left(1 + \frac{2i}{\sqrt{\pi}} \int_0^x e^{t^2}\, dt\right)$$

6. Bernoulli's Conjecture

In 1702 John Bernoulli conjectured that '*the integral of any rational function is expressible in terms of other rational functions, trigonometric functions, and logarithmic functions*'.

Example 6.1: Prove that

$$\int \frac{dx}{1+x^2} = \tan^{-1}x + K$$

Proof: We have

$$\int \frac{dx}{1+x^2} = \int F[x,(1+x^2)]dx = \int F[x, y_1]dx$$

$$\text{where,} \quad \left[\frac{dy_1}{dx} = 2x \in F\right]$$

By strong Liouville theorem

$$\int \frac{dx}{1+x^2} = U_0 + \sum_{j=1}^{n} C_j \log U_j \quad (6.1)$$

On differentiating it we get

$$\frac{1}{1+x^2} = U'_0 + \sum_{j=1}^{n} C_j \frac{U'_j}{U_j}$$

Now

$$U'_0 + \sum_{j=1}^{n} C_j \frac{U'_j}{U_j} = \frac{1}{(1+ix)(1-ix)}$$

$$= \frac{1}{2}\left[\frac{1}{(1+ix)} + \frac{1}{(1-ix)}\right]$$

$$= \frac{1}{2i}\left[\frac{(1+ix)'}{(1+ix)} - \frac{(1-ix)'}{(1-ix)}\right]$$

$$= \frac{1}{2i}\left[\{\log(1+ix)\}' - \{\log(1-ix)\}'\right]$$

where the sign ' denotes differentiation with respect to x. Comparing it with (6.1), we get $U_0' = 0$ therefore, $U_0 = K$ and $C_1 = (1/2i)$, $C_2 = (-1/2i)$, $U_1 = (1+ix)$, $U_2 = (1-ix)$.

Therefore

$$\int \frac{dx}{1+x^2} = \frac{1}{2i}\left[\{\log(1+ix)\} - \{\log(1-ix)\}\right] + K$$

$$= \frac{1}{2i}\log\frac{(1+ix)}{(1-ix)} + K = -\frac{1}{2i}\log\frac{(1-ix)}{(1+ix)} + K$$

$$= \frac{i}{2}\log\frac{(i+x)}{(i-x)} + K = \tan^{-1}x + K.$$

Similarly we can prove the following

$$\int \frac{2x\,dx}{1+x^2} = \ln(1+x^2) + K$$

$$\int \frac{dx}{x^2} = -\frac{1}{x} + K$$

$$\int \left(\frac{1+2x}{1+x^2}\right) = \tan^{-1}x + \ln(1+x^2) + K$$

to show the statement of the Bernoulli's conjecture.

Exercise-6

Prove that the following elementary functions satisfy Bernoulli's Conjecture on integration:

1. $\dfrac{x(x+3)}{x+5}$

2. $\dfrac{(x^3+8)(x-3)}{x^2-2x+4}$

3. $\dfrac{1}{1-2x-x^2}$

4. $\dfrac{1+x^2}{1+x^4}$

7. Laplace's Theorem

In 1812 Laplace found that 'the integral of a rational function of x, e^x and logx is either a rational function of those functions or the sum of such a rational function and of a finite number of constant multiples of logarithms of similar functions'. Based on this fact he stated the following theorem:

Laplace's Theorem: A rational function has an anti-derivative and its integral is always an elementary function.

In general it is composed of two parts: one of a rational function and another transcendental part or logarithmic part.

For example, we can easily prove that

$$\int \frac{x\,dx}{1+x} = x - \ln(1+x)$$

$$\int \frac{(1+x^2)^2 + x}{x(1+x^2)}\,dx = \frac{x^2}{2} + \ln|x| + \frac{i}{2}\ln\left|\frac{x+i}{x-i}\right|.$$

He gave the following conjecture also:

Laplace's Conjecture: The integral of an algebraic function need contain only those algebraic functions which are present in the integrand. This conjecture was later proved by Abel.

For example, we can prove that

$$\int (x^2 + 1)dx = \frac{x^3}{3} + x + K$$

$$\int (x^4 - 6x^3 + 4x^2 - x + 6)dx$$

$$= \frac{x^5}{5} - 6\frac{x^4}{4} + 4\frac{x^3}{3} - \frac{x^2}{2} + 6x + K$$

Exercise-7

Verify Laplace theorem for the following functions:

1. $\dfrac{x^2}{1+x}$

2. $\dfrac{3x+4}{2x^2-8}$

3. $\dfrac{x^2-8x+4}{x^2+4}$

Verify Laplace Conjecture for the functions:

1. $x^4 + 8x^3 + 4$

2. $x^2 + 8x + 3$

3. $4x^3 - 2x + 7$

8. Abel's Theorem

N. H. Abel (1826, 1829) studied the indefinite integrals of general algebraic functions, which later became known as Abel's Integrals. Based on his work he proposed the following theorem:

'If y is an algebraic function of x and if the integral of y is algebraic, the integral is rational in y and x'.

For example: We know that

$$\int x^n \, dx = \frac{x^{n+1}}{n+1}, \text{for } n \neq -1$$

In this integration the integrand is $y = x^n$ and the integral is

$$\frac{x^{n+1}}{n+1} = \frac{y\,x}{n+1}$$

which is rational in y and x.

For the integral

$$\int \sqrt{3x+4} \, dx = \frac{2(3x+4)^{3/2}}{9}$$

the integrand is $y = \sqrt{3x+4}$ and the integral is

$$\frac{2(3x+4)^{3/2}}{9} = \frac{2y^3}{9}$$

which is rational in y and x.

For the integral

$$\int x^2(1+x^3)^{3/2}\,dx = \frac{2(1+x^3)^{5/2}}{15}$$

the integrand is $y = x^2(1+x^3)^{3/2}$ and the integral is

$$\frac{2(1+x^3)^{5/2}}{15} = \frac{2}{15}\frac{y^{5/3}}{x^{10/3}}$$

which is rational in y and x.

Exercise-8

Verify the Abel's theorem for the following algebraic functions:

1. $x^2\sqrt{a^3 + x^3}$ 2. $(2x + 3)\sqrt{x^3 + 3x}$

3. $x^3\sqrt{x^2 + 5}$ 4. $x^3\sqrt{ax^2 + 5}$

5. $(2x^2 + 3)\sqrt{x + 4}$ 6. $(x + 2)\sqrt{2x + 1}$

9. Liouville's Theorems

There is a well established property in differential calculus that 'the derivative of an elementary function is again an elementary function'. Based on this fact in 1833 Joseph Liouville created a framework for constructive integration by finding out when indefinite integrals of elementary functions are again elementary functions. The main results on functions with nonelementary integrals began with Liouville results.

The first problem considered by him in the field of integration in finite terms deals with the integration of general algebraic functions. He introduced a theorem, which is reminiscent of Laplace's theorem, now known as *Liouville's First Theorem on Integration or simply Liouville's theorem,* as stated below:

Liouville's First Theorem on Integration: If an algebraic function is integrable (antiderivable) in finite terms, its antiderivative is the finite sum of an algebraic function and the logarithms of algebraic functions.

In mathematical notation, if f(x) is an algebraic function of x and if

$$\int f(x)\,dx$$

is elementary, then

$$\int f(x)\, dx = U_0 + \sum_{i=1}^{n} C_i \log(U_i)$$

where the C_i's are constants and the U_i's are algebraic functions of x.

In 1835 he generalized this theorem to several variables and gave *Strong Liouville's theorem*, and thereby greatly extended the class of functions one can prove to have nonelementary integrals or indefinite nonintegrable functions.

Strong Liouville's Theorem:

(a) If F is an algebraic function of $x, y_1, y_2, \ldots, y_m$ where $y_1, y_2, \ldots, y_m$ are functions of x, whose derivatives

$$\frac{dy_1}{dx}, \frac{dy_2}{dx}, \frac{dy_3}{dx}, \ldots, \frac{dy_m}{dx}$$

are rational functions of $x, y_1, y_2, \ldots, y_m$, then

$$\int F(x, y_1, y_2, \ldots, y_m)\, dx$$

is elementary if and only if

$$\int F(x, y_1, y_2, \ldots, y_m)\, dx = U_0 + \sum_{j=1}^{n} C_j \log(U_j)$$

where the C_j's are constants, and the U_j's are algebraic functions of $x, y_1, y_2, \ldots, y_m.$

(b) If $F(x, y_1, y_2, \ldots, y_m)$ is a rational function and

$$\frac{dy_1}{dx}, \frac{dy_2}{dx}, \frac{dy_3}{dx}, \dots, \frac{dy_m}{dx}$$

are rational functions of $x, y_1, y_2, \dots, y_m$, then the U_j's in part (a) must be rational functions of $x, y_1, y_2, \dots, y_m$.

Thereafter in the same year 1835 he found the special case of this theorem, which gives the necessary and sufficient conditions for the existence of elementary function of some special functions.

Strong Liouville's Theorem (Special Case):

If f(x) and g(x) are rational functions with g(x) non-constant, then

$$\int f(x)\, e^{g(x)}\, dx$$

is elementary if and only if there exists a rational function R(x) such that

$$f(x) = R'(x) + R(x)\, g'(x).$$

For any such R(x), $R(x)\, e^{g(x)}$ is an elementary antiderivative of f(x).

By applying the above theorems, he proved that the following integrals

$$\int e^{x^2}\, dx, \int e^{-x^2}\, dx, \int \frac{e^x}{x}\, dx, \int \frac{e^{-x}}{x}\, dx,$$

$$\int \frac{sinx}{x}\, dx, \int \frac{cosx}{x}\, dx, \int \frac{dx}{logx}$$

can not be expressed in terms of elementary functions i.e., they are indefinite nonintegrable functions or nonelementary functions or nonelementary integrals.

In fact, he proved that some integrals such as

$$\int_0^x e^{-t^2}\, dt,$$

$$\int_0^x (1 - m\, sin^2 t)^{-1/2}\, dt$$

can not be expressed in terms of a finite number of elementary functions. They were thus the first integration problem which seemed impossible to properly solve in the sense of Leibniz.

He showed also that the elliptic integrals of the first and second kinds have no elementary expressions. By 1841, Liouville had developed a theory of integration that settled the question of integration in finite terms for many important cases.

Due to the wide applications of Liouville theorem, let us apply these theorems in evaluating the indefinite integrals to show that when an elemenetary function is elementary (indefinite integrable) or nonelementary (indefinite nonintegrable) functions or antiderivable or nonelementary integrals.

Solved Examples

Example-9.1: Prove that the integral

$$\int \frac{e^{x^2+bx+c}}{2x+b}\,dx$$

is nonelementary.

Proof: Using special case of strong Liouville theorem, we know that the above indefinite integral is elementary (integrable in indefinite integral case) if and only if there exists a rational function R(x) such that

$$R'(x) + (2x+b)R(x) = \frac{1}{(2x+b)} \qquad \text{(i)}$$

Let $R(x) = \frac{p(x)}{q(x)}$, where gcd $(p(x), q(x)) = 1$.

Then from (i) we have

$$\frac{q(x)p'(x) - p(x)q'(x) + (2x+b)p(x)q(x)}{[q(x)]^2} = \frac{1}{(2x+b)} \qquad \text{(ii)}$$

$$\Rightarrow (2x+b)q(x)p'(x) - (2x+b)p(x)q'(x) + (2x+b)^2 p(x)q(x)$$
$$= [q(x)]^2$$

$$\Rightarrow (2x+b)p'(x) - q(x) + (2x+b)^2 p(x) = \frac{(2x+b)p(x)q'(x)}{q(x)}$$

Which implies that q(x) divides (2x+b), since q(x) cannot divide p(x) and $q'(x)$. So either q(x) is a constant k or k (2x+b).

When $q(x) = k$, from (ii) we have

$$\frac{kp'(x) + (2x + b)p(x)k}{[k]^2} = \frac{1}{(2x + b)}$$

$$\Rightarrow p'(x) + (2x + b)p(x) = \frac{k}{(2x + b)}$$

$$\Rightarrow (2x + b)p'(x) + (2x + b)^2p(x) = k \quad (iii)$$

Comparing the degrees of x in both sides of (iii), we get that the degree of x in right hand side is 0, whereas the degree of x in left hand side is greater than or equal to 2 for any polynomial p(x), which results out in a contradiction. So q(x) cannot be a constant.

When q(x) = k (2x+b), then from (ii) we have

$$\frac{k(2x + b)p'(x) - p(x)2k + k(2x + b)^2p(x)}{[k(2x + b)]^2} = \frac{1}{(2x + b)}$$

$$\Rightarrow (2x + b)p'(x) - p(x)2 + (2x + b)^2p(x) = k(2x + b) \quad (iv)$$

Again comparing the degrees of x in both sides of (iv), we get a contradiction. Thus we conclude that no such R(x) exists. Therefore the given integral is nonelementary.

Example-9.2: Prove that the integral

$$\int \frac{e^z dz}{1 - z}$$

is nonelementary.

Proof: We have on putting 1 - z = p

$$\int \frac{e^z dz}{1-z} = -e \int \frac{e^{-p} dp}{p}$$

From strong Liouville's theorem (special case), it is elementary if and only if there exists a rational function R(p) such that

$$\frac{1}{p} = R'(p) - R(p) \qquad \text{(i)}$$

Let

$$R(p) = \frac{P(p)}{Q(p)}$$

where gcd $(P, Q) = 1$. Then from (i) we have

$$\{Q(p)\}^2 = pQ(p)P'(p) - pP(p)Q'(p) - P(p)Q(p) \quad \text{(ii)}$$

$$\Rightarrow pP'(p) - Q(p) - pP(p) = \frac{pP(p)Q'(p)}{Q(p)}$$

Which implies that Q(p) divides p, because Q(p) cannot divide P(p) and Q'(p), which means that Q(p) = k or Q(p) = k p, where k is a constant.

When Q(p) = k, from (ii) we have

$$pP'(p) - pP(p) = k \quad \text{(iii)}$$

Comparing the degrees of p on both side results out in a contradiction. Hence $Q(p) \neq k$.

When Q(p) = k p, then from (ii) we have

$$pk = pP'(p) - (1 - p)P(p)$$

Which is not true for any polynomial P(p). Thus we conclude that such R(p) does not exist i. e., this integral is nonelementary.

Example-9.3: Prove that the integral

$$\int \frac{e^z \, dz}{(1 + z^2)}$$

is nonelementary.

Proof: We have

$$\int \frac{e^z \, dz}{(1 + z^2)}$$

$$= \frac{1}{2}\left[\int \frac{e^z \, dz}{(1 + iz)} + \int \frac{e^z \, dz}{(1 - iz)}\right]$$

Now on putting $1 + i\, z = p$, we get

$$\int \frac{e^z \, dz}{(1 + iz)} = \frac{e^i}{i}\int \frac{e^{-ip} \, dp}{p}$$

By strong Liouville's theorem (special case), it is elementary if and only if there exists a rational function R(x) which satisfies the identity

$$\frac{1}{p} = R'(p) - iR(p)$$

$$\Rightarrow \frac{1}{p} = R'(p) \text{ or } R(p) = 0$$

But R(p) cannot be zero, so such R(p) does not exist. Hence it is nonelementary integral.

Also on putting $1 - i\,z = p$, we get

$$\int \frac{e^z\, dz}{(1 - iz)} = ie^{-i} \int \frac{e^{ip}\, dp}{p}$$

Again by strong Liouville's theorem (special case), it is elementary if and only if there exists a rational function R(x) which satisfies the identity

$$\frac{1}{p} = R'(p) + i\,R(p)$$

$$\Rightarrow \frac{1}{p} = R'(p) \text{ or } R(p) = 0$$

But R(p) cannot be zero, so such R(p) does not exist. Hence it is nonelementary. Therefore the given integral is nonelementary.

Example-9.4: Show that the integral

$$\int \frac{e^{ax^2 + b}}{x}\, dx, \ a \neq 0$$

is nonelementary.

Proof: We have

$$\int \frac{e^{ax^2+b}}{x}dx = \int \frac{e^{ax^2}}{x}dx + \int \frac{e^b}{x}dx$$

$$= e^b \log x + \int \frac{2axe^{ax^2}}{2ax^2}dx$$

Now putting $ax^2 = z$ we get

$$\int \frac{2axe^{ax^2}}{2ax^2}dx = \frac{1}{2}\int \frac{e^z}{z}dz = \frac{1}{2}\int z^{-1}e^z dz$$

which is nonelementary as discussed earlier. Hence the given integral is nonelementary.

Example-9.5: Show that the integral

$$\int \frac{e^{\sin x}}{\cos x}dx$$

is nonelementary.

Proof: We have $\int \frac{e^{\sin x}}{\cos x}dx = \int \frac{e^{\sin x}\cos x}{\cos^2 x}dx$

On putting $\sin x = z$, we get

$$\int \frac{e^{\sin x}\cos x}{\cos^2 x}dx = \int \frac{e^z dz}{(1-z^2)}$$

which is nonelementary as proved earlier. Hence the given integral is nonelementary.

Example-9.6: Show that the integral

$$\int \frac{e^{\sin x^2}}{2x.\cos x^2}\, dx$$

is nonelementary.

Proof: We have on putting $\sin x^2 = z$,

$$\int \frac{e^{\sin x^2}}{2x.\cos x^2}\, dx = \int \frac{e^z dz}{4(1-z^2)\sin^{-1} z}$$

$$= \int F\!\left(z, e^z, \sqrt{1-z^2}, \sin^{-1} z\right) dz$$

$$= \int F\!\left(z, y_1, y_2, y_3\right) dz$$

By strong Liouville's theorem, it is elementary if and only if there exists an identity containing U_j a function of z, y_1, y_2, and y_3 of the form

$$\frac{dU_0}{dz} + \sum_{i=1}^{n} C_i \frac{U'_i}{U_i} = \frac{e^z}{(1-z^2)\sin^{-1} z}$$

Taking different possible forms of U_j like

$$e^z \log \sin^{-1} z, \, e^z \sqrt{1-z^2} \, \log \sin^{-1} z$$

etc., we find that no such U_j exist. Hence the given integral is nonelementary.

Example-9.7: Show that the integral

$$\int \frac{e^{x^2+x}}{(x+1)}\,dx$$

is nonelementary.

Proof: Applying strong Liouville's theorem (special case), we find that the integral

$$\int \frac{e^{x^2+x}}{(x+1)}\,dx$$

is elementary if and only if there exists a rational function R(x), which satisfies an identity of the form

$$\frac{1}{(x+1)} = R'(x) + (2x+1)R(x) \tag{i}$$

Let

$$R(x) = \frac{p(x)}{q(x)}$$

where gcd(p(x), q(x))=1.

Then from (i) we have

$$(x + 1)q(x)p'(x) - (x + 1)p(x)q'(x) + (2x + 1)(x + 1)p(x)q(x)$$
$$= [q(x)]^2$$

$$\Rightarrow (x + 1)p'(x) - q(x) + (2x + 1)(x + 1)p(x)$$
$$= \frac{(x + 1)p(x)q'(x)}{q(x)} \qquad (ii)$$

which implies that q(x) divides (x+1) i.e., either $q(x) = k$ a constant or $q(x) = k \, (x+1)$.

When $q(x) = k$, we have from (ii)

$$(x+1)p'(x) - k + (2x+1)(x+1)p(x) = 0$$
$$\Rightarrow (x+1)p'(x) + (2x+1)(x+1)p(x) = k$$

Comparing the degrees of x in both sides, we get a contradiction. Therefore q(x) cannot be a constant.

When $q(x) = k(x+1)$, we have from (ii)

$$(x+1)p'(x) - k(x+1) + (2x+1)(x+1)p(x) = p(x)$$

Again comparing the degrees of x in both sides, we get a contradiction. Therefore we find that q(x) cannot be equal to k (x+1). Finally we conclude that no such R(x) exist. Hence the given integral is nonelementary.

Example-9.8: Show that the integral

$$\int \frac{e^{x^3+2x^2+x}}{x^2+2x+1}\,dx$$

is nonelementary.

Proof: Applying strong Liouville's theorem (special case), we find that the integral

$$\int \frac{e^{x^3+2x^2+x}}{x^2+2x+1}\,dx$$

is elementary if and only if there exists a rational function R(x), which satisfies an identity of the form

$$\frac{1}{(x^2+2x+1)} = R'(x) + (3x^2+4x+1)R(x) \quad \text{(i)}$$

Let

$$R(x) = \frac{p(x)}{q(x)}$$

Where gcd(p(x), q(x))=1. Then from (i) we have

$$q(x)p'(x) - p(x)q'(x) + (3x^2 + 4x + 1)p(x)q(x)$$

$$= \left(\frac{q(x)}{x+1}\right)^2 \qquad \text{(ii)}$$

Which implies that q(x) = (x+1) r(x) for some polynomial r(x). Putting it in (ii), we get

$$(x+1)r(x)p'(x) - p(x)r(x) - (x+1)p(x)r'(x)$$
$$+ (3x^2 + 4x + 1)(x+1)p(x)r(x) = \{r(x)\}^2 \quad \text{(ii)}$$

$$(x+1)p'(x) - p(x) - r(x) + (3x^2 + 4x + 1)(x+1)p(x)$$
$$= \left(\frac{(x+1)p(x)r'(x)}{r(x)}\right)^2$$

But r(x) cannot divide p(x) as q(x) cannot divide p(x), which implies that r(x) divides r'(x) or (x+1). When r(x) divides r'(x), it means that r(x) is a constant. Then we have from (iii)

$$k(x+1)p'(x) - kp(x) + (3x^2 + 4x + 1)(x+1)p(x)k = k^2$$

$$\Rightarrow (x+1)p'(x) - p(x) + (3x^2 + 4x + 1)(x+1)p(x) = k$$

Comparing the degrees of x in both sides now results out in a contradiction. Therefore r(x) cannot be a constant. When r(x) divides (x+1), let r(x)=k(x+1). Then from (iii) we have

$$k(x+1)^2 p'(x) + (3x^2 + 4x + 1)(x+1)^2 p(x)k = k^2(x+1)^2$$
$$\Rightarrow p'(x) + (3x^2 + 4x + 1)p(x) = k$$

comparing the degrees of x in both sides again results out in a contradiction. Therefore r(x) cannot be equal to k(x+1). Finally we conclude that no such R(x) exist. Hence the given integral is nonelementary.

Example-9.9: Show that the integral

$$\int \frac{\sin x}{x}\, dx$$

is nonelementary.

Proof: We have using Euler's identity

$$\int \frac{\sin x}{x}\, dx = img\left[\int \frac{e^{ix}}{x}\, dx \right]$$

Taking $g(x) = ix$, $f(x) = 1/x$, and applying strong Liouville's theorem (special case), we find that it is elementary if and only if there exists a rational function $R(x)$ which satisfies the identity

$$R'(x) + iR(x) = \frac{1}{x} \Rightarrow R'(x) = \frac{1}{x} \ \& \ R(x) = 0$$

which is impossible. Hence the given integral is nonelementary.

Example-9.10: Show that the integral

$$\int \frac{\tan x}{x}\, dx$$

is nonelementary.

Proof: We have

$$\int \frac{\tan x}{x}\, dx = \int \frac{\sec x \tan x}{x \sec x}\, dx$$

On putting secx = z, it becomes

$$= \int \frac{dz}{z \sec^{-1} z} = \int \frac{\sqrt{z^2 - 1}\, dz}{z\sqrt{z^2 - 1} \sec^{-1} z}$$

$$= \int F\left[z, \sqrt{z^2 - 1}, \sec^{-1} z \right] dz$$

$$= \int F[z, y_1, y_2]\, dz$$

$$\left[\frac{dy_1}{dz} = \frac{z}{\sqrt{z^2 - 1}} = \frac{z}{y_1}, \frac{dy_2}{dz} = \frac{1}{z y_1} \right]$$

By strong Liouville's theorem, it is elementary if and only if there exists an identity of the form

$$\frac{1}{z \sec^{-1} z} = U_0' + \sum_{i=1}^{n} C_i \frac{U_i'}{U_i}$$

But no such U_j exist. Hence the given integral is nonelementary.

Example-9.11: Show that the integral

$$\int \frac{\tan x}{(ax^3 + x^2 + b)}\, dx$$

is nonelementary.

Proof: We have

$$\int \frac{\tan x}{(ax^3 + x^2 + b)}\, dx = \int \frac{\sec x \tan x}{(ax^3 + x^2 + b)\sec x}\, dx$$

On putting secx=z, it becomes

$$= \int \frac{dz}{(ax^3 + x^2 + b)z} = \int \frac{dz}{z\left[a(\sec^{-1} z)^3 + (\sec^{-1} z)^2 + b\right]}$$

$$= \int F[z, \sqrt{z^2 - 1}, \sec^{-1} z]dz = \int F[z, y_1, y_2]dz$$

$$\left[\frac{dy_1}{dz} = \frac{z}{\sqrt{z^2 - 1}} = \frac{z}{y_1}, \frac{dy_2}{dz} = \frac{1}{zy_1}\right]$$

By strong Liouville's theorem, it is elementary if and only if there exists an identity of the form

$$\frac{1}{z[a(\sec^{-1} z)^3 + (\sec c^{-1}z) + b]} = U_0' + \sum_{i=1}^{n} C_i \frac{U_i'}{U_i}$$

Giving different values of a and b, we can find that no such U_j exist. Hence the given integral is nonelementary.

Example-9.12: Show that the integral

$$\int e^{x^2} dx$$

is nonelementary.

Proof: By strong Liouville's theorem (special case) this integral is elementary if and only if there exists a rational function R(x) such that

$$1 = R'(x) + 2xR(x) \qquad \text{(i)}$$

Let

$$R(x) = \frac{p(x)}{q(x)}, \text{ where } \gcd\{p(x), q(x)\} = 1.$$

Then from (i) we have

$$p'(x) - q(x) + 2xp(x) = \frac{p(x)q'(x)}{q(x)}$$

which implies that q(x) divides q'(x) i. e., q(x) is a constant. Without loss of generality, we can assume that R(x)=p(x). Then from (i) we have

$$1 = p'(x) + 2xp(x) \qquad \text{(ii)}$$

where p(x) is a polynomial of degree ≥ 1. Comparing the degrees of x on both sides of (ii) now results out in a contradiction. Hence such R(x) does not exist i. e., the given integral is nonelementary.

Exercise-9

Prove that the following integrals are nonelementary:

1. $\int \frac{e^z dz}{1+z}$ 2. $\int \frac{e^z\, dz}{z^2(z^2-1)}$ 3. $\int \frac{e^{\cos x}}{-\sin x}\, dx$

4. $\int e^{\sin x}\, dx$ 5. $\int e^{\tan x}\, dx$ 6. $\int e^{\sinh x}\, dx$

10. Chebyshev's Theorem

In 1853 P. L. Chebyshev worked in the area of integration on specific forms of algebraic functions closely associated with the work of *Abel* and *Liouville* and presented the following theorem:

P. L. Chebyshev's Theorem: If p, q, and r are rational numbers and a, b are real numbers with $a, b, r \neq 0$, then

$$\int x^p (a + bx^r)^q \, dx$$

is elementary if and only if at least one of

$$\frac{p+1}{r}, q \; or \; \frac{p+1}{r+q}$$

is an integer.

Based on the above theorem he showed that the following integrals

$$\int (1 + x^2)^{1/2} \, dx, \int \sqrt{1 + x^3} \, dx,$$

$$\int \sqrt{1 + x^{-4}} \, dx, \int \sqrt{\sin x} \, dx, \int \sqrt{\cos x} \, dx$$

are nonelementary.

He also found the following corollaries from the above theorem:

Chebyshev's Corollary: If m and n are integers, then

$$\int (1 - x^n)^{1/m}\, dx$$

is elementary if and only if $m = \pm 1$, or $n = \pm 1$, or $m = n = 2$, or $m = -n$.

Based on the above corollary he showed that following integrals

$$\int \sin^m x \, \cos^m x \, dx, \quad \int \sqrt{\tan x}\, dx$$

are elementary.

Chebyshev's Integral: He also showed that the integral

$$u = \int x^p (1 - x)^q\, dx$$

where each of p and q is rational and not zero, to be elementary, it is necessary and sufficient that at least one of p, q and p + q be an integer.

Example 10.1: Find out whether the integral

$$\int x^4(1-x)^3\,dx$$

is elementary or nonelementary?

Solution: Comparing this integral from the Chebyshev integral, we find that p = 4 and q = 3. Here all p, q and p + q = 7 are integers, therefore it will be elementary.

Also we know that every algebraic function has antiderivative. Therefore it is elementary.

Excerice-10

Find out which of the following integrals is (are) elementary or nonelementary:

1. $\int x^6(1-x)^4\,dx$ 2. $\int x^3(2+3x^2)^4\,dx$

3. $\int \sqrt{cotx}\,dx$ 4. $\int \sqrt{1-x^{-4}}\,dx$

5. $\int \sqrt{1+x^{-6}}\,dx$ 6. $\int \sqrt{1-x^3}\,dx$

11. Liouville Hardy's Theorem

In 1905 G. H. Hardy found another special case of the strong Liouville theorem known as:

Liouville-Hardy Theorem: If f(x) is a rational function, then

$$\int f(x)\,\log x\,dx$$

is elementary if and only if there exists a rational function g(x) and a constant C such that

$$f(x) = \frac{C}{x} + g'(x).$$

Example 11.1: Verify the Liouville-Hardy theorem for the following integral

$$\int \frac{\log x}{x^2}\,dx$$

Solution: Putting $\log x = z$, we get

$$\int \frac{\log x}{x^2}\,dx = \int \frac{z\,e^z}{e^{2z}}\,dz = \int z\,e^{-z}\,dz$$

$$= e^{-z}(1-z) = \frac{(1-z)}{e^z}$$

$$= \frac{(1-\log x)}{x} + K$$

Verification: Let us suppose that there exists a rational function g(x) and a constant C such that

$$f(x) = \frac{C}{x} + g'(x)$$

$$\text{i.e.,} \quad \frac{1}{x^2} = \frac{C}{x} + g'(x)$$

$$\Rightarrow \frac{1 - Cx}{x^2} = g'(x)$$

Integrating both sides we get

$$g(x) = \int \frac{1 - Cx}{x^2}\, dx$$

$$= -\frac{1}{x} - C \log x$$

which verifies the Liouville-Hardy theorem.

Based on this theorem he showed that the integrals

$$\int \frac{\log x\, dx}{(x - a)}, a \neq 0$$

$$\int \frac{\log x\, dx}{(x^2 + 1)}, \int (\sec^{-1} x)^2\, dx$$

are nonelementary. In 1916 he has also written that the standard elliptic integrals

$$\int \frac{dx}{\sqrt{(1 - x^2)(1 - k^2 x^2)}}, \int \frac{\sqrt{(1 - x^2)}\, dx}{\sqrt{(1 - k^2 x^2)}},$$

$$\int \frac{dx}{\sqrt{4x^3 - ax - b}}$$

are not expressible in terms of elementary functions.

Exercise-11

Verify the Lioville-Hardy theorem for the following integrals:

(i) $\int \frac{\log x}{x} dx$ $\qquad$ $[g(x) = (1 - C) \log x]$

(ii) $\int \log x \, dx$ $\qquad$ $[g(x) = x - C \log x]$

(iii) $\int x^2 \log x \, dx$

12. Two Special Properties

In 1994 in an invitation paper **E. A. Marchisotto & G. A. Zakeri** mentioned two important properties as examples obtained from the special case of strong Liouville's theorem, which are very useful in deciding the elementary and nonelementary functions:

Property 1: $\int x^{2n} e^{ax^2} dx$ for n an integer, is non-elementary for $a \neq 0$.

For n = 0 and a = -1, this is the error function. Using the above property, it can be proved that the following integrals are nonelementary:

$$\int \sqrt{logx}\, dx = \int 2t^2 e^{t^2} dt$$

$$\int \frac{dx}{\sqrt{logx}} = \int 2 e^{t^2} dt$$

$$\int \frac{e^{ax} dx}{\sqrt{x}} = \int 2 e^{at^2} dt$$

Property 2: $\int x^{-n} e^{ax} dx$ for n a positive integer and a a nonzero constant, is nonelementary.

Using these properties, following integrals can be proved nonelementary:

$$\int e^{e^x}\, dx = \int \frac{e^t}{t}\, dt$$

$$\int \frac{dx}{logx} = \int \frac{e^t}{t}\, dt$$

$$\int log\,(logx)\, dx = xlog(logx) - \int \frac{dx}{logx}$$

$$\int \frac{sinx}{x}\, dx = Img\left(\int \frac{e^{ix}}{x}\, dx\right)$$

In 1994 they proved also that the following integrals are nonelementary

$$\int x^x\, dx, \int x^{-x}\, dx, \int x^x\, logx\, dx\,,$$

$$\int \sqrt{sinx}\, dx, \int \sqrt{cosx}\, dx$$

Solved Examples

Example-12.1: Show that the integral

$$\int \frac{e^{tan\,x}}{sec^2 x}\, dx$$

is nonelementary.

Proof: We have, on putting $tanx = z$

$$\int \frac{e^{\tan x}}{\sec^2 x}\,dx = \int \frac{e^z}{(1+z^2)^2}\,dz = \frac{1}{4}\int \frac{e^z dz}{(iz)(1-iz)^2} - \frac{1}{4}\int \frac{e^z dz}{(iz)(1+iz)^2} \qquad (i)$$

On putting $1-iz=p$ in the first integral of (i)

$$\int \frac{e^z dz}{(iz)(1-iz)^2} = ie^{-i}\left[\int \frac{e^{ip}dp}{(1-p)} + \int \frac{e^{ip}dp}{p} + \int \frac{e^{ip}dp}{p^2}\right] \qquad (ii)$$

where the second and third integrals are nonelementary from Property-2. Now putting $1-p=X$ in the first integral of (ii) we have

$$\int \frac{e^{ip}dp}{(1-p)} = -e^i \int \frac{e^{-iX}dX}{X}$$

which is nonelementary from Property-2. Hence the first integral of (i) is nonelementary. Similarly we can prove that the second integral of (i) is also nonelementary. Therefore the given integral is nonelementary.

Example-12.2: Show that the integral

$$\int \frac{e^{\sin^2 x}}{\sin 2x}\,dx$$

is nonelementary.

Proof: We have on putting $\sin^2 x = z$,

$$\int \frac{e^{\sin^2 x}}{\sin 2x}\,dx = \frac{1}{4}\int \frac{e^z dz}{z(1-z^2)}$$

$$= \frac{1}{4}\left[\int \frac{ze^z dz}{(1-z^2)} + \int \frac{e^z dz}{z} \right]$$

Where $\int \frac{e^z}{z} dz$ is nonelementary from Property-2.

Now since $\int \frac{ze^z}{(1-z^2)} dz = \frac{1}{2}\int \frac{e^z dz}{(1-z)} - \frac{1}{2}\int \frac{e^z dz}{(1+z)}$

where, $\int \frac{e^z dz}{(1-z)} = -e \int \frac{e^{-p}}{p} dp$, on putting 1-z=p, which is nonelementary and

$$\int \frac{e^z dz}{(1+z)} = \frac{1}{e}\int \frac{e^p}{p} dp$$

on putting $1+z = p$, which is also nonelementary, from Property-2. Hence the given integral is nonelementary.

Example-12.3: Show that the integral

$$\int \frac{\cosh x}{x} dx$$

is nonelementary.

Proof: We have

$$\int \frac{\cosh x}{x} dx = \frac{1}{2}\int \frac{e^x}{x} dx + \frac{1}{2}\int \frac{e^{-x}}{x} dx$$

Both are well proved nonelementary functions follow from Property-2. Therefore the given integral is nonelementary.

Example-12.4: Show that the integral

$$\int e^{-x^2}\,dx$$

is nonelementary.

Proof: It is a well proved nonelementary integral. It follows also from Property-1.

Example-12.5: Show that the integral

$$\int \sin(x^2 + 3)\,dx$$

is nonelementary.

Proof: We have

$$\int \sin(x^2 + 3)\,dx = \frac{1}{2i}\left[\int e^{i(x^2+3)}\,dx - \int e^{-i(x^2+3)}\,dx\right]$$

Both are nonelementary by Property-1.

Alternative Proof: By strong Liouville's theorem (special case) the first integral $\int e^{i(x^2+3)}\,dx$ is elementary if and only if there exists a rational function R(x) such that

$$1 = R\,'(x) + i2xR(x)$$

$$\Rightarrow R'(x) = 1 \text{ and } xR(x) = 0$$

But such R(x) cannot exist, which satisfies both conditions. Hence this is nonelementary. Similarly we can proof that the second integral $\int e^{-i(x^2+3)} dx$ is nonelementary. Therefore the given integral is also nonelementary.

Exercise-12

Prove the following integrals are nonelementary:

$$1. \int x^6 e^{2x^2} dx \qquad 2. \int x^4 e^{3x^2} dx$$

$$3. \int x^{-4} e^{2x} dx \qquad 4. \int x^{-3} e^{-4x} dx$$

13. Inverse Function Theorem

In 1994 in an invitation paper **E. A. Marchisotto & G. A. Zakeri** also discussed the inverse function theorem, which was known to Liouville (1841) in writing his paper on Riccati equation. It also appears in the works of F. D. Parker (1955), J. H. Staib (1966), and in a recent note by E. Key (1994). It states that:

Inverse Function Theorem: Let f(x) and f $^{-1}$(x) be inverses of one another on some closed interval [a, b]. If f(x) and f $^{-1}$(x) are elementary functions over [a, b], then $\int f(x)\, dx$ is elementary if and only if $\int f^{-1}(x)\, dx$ is elementary.

For example, the integral $\int \sqrt{logx}\, dx$ is nonelementary since the integral of the inverse function of its integrand $\int e^{x^2}\, dx$ is nonelementary and the integral $\int \frac{dx}{logx}$ is nonelementary since $\int e^{1/x}\, dx$ is nonelementary.

Exercise-13

Prove that the following functions and their inverses are nonelementary:

1. e^{-x^2} and $\sqrt{\log\left(\frac{1}{x}\right)}$

2. e^{1/x^2} and $\sqrt{\frac{1}{\log x}}$

3. $e^{x^{3/2}}$ and $(\log x)^{2/3}$

4. $\sin\left(\frac{1}{x}\right)$ and $\frac{1}{\sin^{-1} x}$

14. Conjectures

The first example which leads us beyond the region of elementary functions is the *elliptic integrals*. In general, they cannot be expressed in terms of elementary functions.

The first reported study of such integrals was due to **John Wallis (1655)**, when he began to study the arc length of an ellipse. It is a function f(x) which can be expressed in the form

$$f(x) = \int_{c}^{x} R\left(t, \sqrt{P(t)}\right) dt = \int R\left(x, \sqrt{P(x)}\right) dx$$

where R is a rational function of its two arguments, P is a polynomial of degree 3 or 4 with no repeated roots, and c is a constant. Exceptions to this general rule are when P has repeated roots, or when $R(x, y)$ contains no odd powers of y.

Euler also studied elliptic functions and discovered that they were not integrable in terms of elementary functions. Such integrals cannot be evaluated in terms of the elementary functions was finally proved by **Liouville** in 1833.

A. M. Legendre (**1825**) showed that the integration of the three integrals

$$\int \frac{dx}{\sqrt{1-x^2}\,\sqrt{1-k^2x^2}}, \quad \int \frac{x^2dx}{\sqrt{1-x^2}\,\sqrt{1-k^2x^2}},$$

$$\int \frac{dx}{(x-a)\sqrt{1-x^2}\,\sqrt{1-k^2x^2}}$$

where $k^2 \neq 0, 1$ (known as elliptic integrals of the first, second, and third kinds respectively) don't have an antiderivative which can be expressed in terms of the standard functions of calculus. **Conrad** has mentioned that the elliptic integrals of the form $\int \frac{dx}{\sqrt{P(x)}}$ for polynomials P(x) with degree >2 and no double roots, are not integrable.

R. Courant (**1935**) mentioned that attempts to express general integrals of

$$\int \frac{dx}{\sqrt{\left(a_0 + a_1x + a_2x^2 + \ldots\ldots + a_nx^n\right)}},$$

$$\int \sqrt{\left(a_0 + a_1x + a_2x^2 + \ldots\ldots + a_nx^n\right)}\,dx, \quad \int \frac{e^x}{x}dx$$

in terms of elementary functions have always ended in failure.

Following the works of the pioneers of Integral Calculus especially of Nonelementary or Nonintegrable Functions, Yadav (2012) has propounded six types of *nonelementary integrals* as conjectures. He used the term 'conjectures' because he has proved them nonelementary only for particular cases. The proof for higher degree or other possible cases are still open for further research.

Conjecture-1: An indefinite integral of the form

$$\int \frac{e^{f(x)}}{f'(x)}\, dx$$

where f(x) is a polynomial of degree ≥ 2, or a trigonometric (not inverse trigonometric) function, or a hyperbolic (not inverse hyperbolic) function is always nonelementary.

Conjecture-2: An indefinite integral of the form

$$\int \frac{e^{f(x)}}{g(x)}\, dx$$

where f(x) and g(x) are polynomial functions in x of degree greater than or equal to 1, is always nonelementary.

Conjecture-3: An indefinite integral of the form

$$\int \frac{f(x)}{g(x)}\, dx$$

where f(x) is a trigonometric (not inverse trigonometric) function, or a hyperbolic (not inverse hyperbolic) function, and g(x) is a polynomial of degree greater than or equal to 1, is always nonelementary.

Conjecture-4: An indefinite integral of the form

$$\int e^{f(x)}dx$$

where f(x) is a trigonometric (not inverse trigonometric) function, or a hyperbolic (not inverse hyperbolic) function, or a polynomial of degree greater than or equal to 2, is always nonelementary.

Conjecture-5: An indefinite integral of the form

$$\int g[f(x)]dx$$

where f(x) is a polynomial of degree greater than or equal to 2 and g(x) is a trigonometric (not inverse trigonometric) or a hyperbolic (not inverse hyperbolic) function is always nonelementary.

Conjecture-6: An indefinite integral of the form

$$\int \frac{f(x).g(x)}{h(x)}dx$$

where f(x), h(x) are polynomials in x (degree of h(x) is greater than the degree of f(x)) and g(x) is a trigonometric (not inverse trigonometric) or a hyperbolic (not inverse hyperbolic) function is always nonelementary.

References

Baccala B. (**2006**), Risch Integration, University of Maryland, http://www.free soft.org/Classes/ Risch2006/, Spring 2006

Baddoura M. J. (**1994**), Integration in Finite Terms with Elementary Functions and Dilogarithms, **Ph. D. Thesis**, Massachusetts Institute of Technology, January

Baccala B. (**2006**), Risch Integration, University of Maryland, http://www.free soft.org/Classes/ Risch2006/, Spring 2006

Beaumont J, **Bradford** R. & **Davenport** J. H. (**2003**), Better Simplification of Elementary Functions Through Power Series, Proceeding of ISSAC'03, August 3-6, 2003, Philadelphia, Pennsylvania, USA, pp.1-7

Bronstein M. (**2005**), Symbolic Integration I, Transcendental Functions, Chapter-5, Springer, www.springer.com/978-3-540-21493-9, pp.129-180

Churchill R. C. (**2006**), Liouville's Theorem on Integration in Terms of Elementary Functions, Corrected & Extended Version, Kolchin Seminar on Differential Algebra, Hunter College, CUNY, 1-26

Conrad B., Impossibility Theorems for Elementary Integration, University of Michigan, Ann Arbor, MI 48109-1043, pp.1-13

Goetz P. (**2009**), Why certain integrals are impossible, Sonoma State University, March 11, 1-20

Hardy G. H. (**1916**), The Integration of Functions of a Single Variable, 2nd Ed., Cambridge University Press, London, Reprint 1928, pp.1-62

Kaltofen E. (**1984**), A Note on the Risch Differential Equation, Corrected Version of a paper Published in the Proceedings EUROSAM'84, Springer Lecture Notes in Computer Science 174, pp.359-366

Leerawat U. & **Laohakosol** V. (**2002**), A Generalization of Liouville's theorem on Integration in Finite Terms, J. Korean Math. Soc.39(1), pp.13-30

Marchisotto E. A. & **Zakeri** G. A. (**1994**), An Invitation to Integration in Finite Terms, The College Mathematics Journal, Mathematical Association of America, Vol.25, No.4, Sep., pp.295-308

Neubacher A. (**1992**), An Introduction to the Symbolic Integration of Elementary Functions, **Diploma Thesis**, Research Institute of Symbolic Computation, Johannes Kepler University, Linz, Austria, Europe, November, pp.1-97

Risch R. H. (**1969**), The Problem of Integration in Finite Terms, Transactions of the American Mathematical Society, 139: 167-189

Risch R. H. (**1970**), The Solution of the Problem of Integration in Finite Terms, Bulletin of the American Mathematical Society, 76(3), 605-608

Ritt J. F. (**1927**), On the Integration in Finite Terms of Linear Differential Equations of the Second Order, p.51-57

Ritt J. F. (**1948**), Integration in Finite Terms: Liouville's Theory of Elementary Methods, Columbia University Press, New York, pp.1-98

Rosenlicht M. (**1968**), Liouville's Theorem on Functions with Elementary Integrals, Pacific Journal of Mathematics, Vol.24, No.1, p.153-161

Rosenlicht M. (**1972**), Integration in Finite Terms, The American Mathematical Monthly, Vol.79, No.9, November, p.963-972

Rothstein M. (**1976**), Aspects of Symbolic Integration and Simplification of Exponential & Primitive Functions, **Ph. D. Thesis**, University of Wisconsin-Madison, pp.1-104

Singer M. F., **Saunders** B. D. & **Caviness** B. F. (**1985**), An Extension of Liouville's Theorem on Integration in Finite Terms, SIAM J. Comput., Society for Industrial and Applied Mathematics, Vol.14, No.4, Nov., pp.966-990

Trager B. M. (**1984**), Integration of Algebraic Functions, **Ph. D. Thesis**, Massachusetts Institute of Technology, September, pp.1-81

Yadav D. K. **(2007),** General Study on Non-integrable Functions in Indefinite Integral Case, **International Research Journal**, **Acta Ciencia Indica**, Vol.33M, No.4, 1667-1670, Pragati Prakashan, U.P., INDIA

Yadav D. K. & **Sen** D. K. **(2008),** Revised Paper on Indefinite Nonintegrable Functions, **International Research Journal**, **Acta Ciencia Indica**, Vol.34 M, No.3, 1383-1384, **2008**, Pragati Prakashan, U.P., INDIA

Yadav D. K. & **Sen** D. K. **(2013)**, Proof of First Standard Form of Non-elementary Functions, **I. J. of Advanced Research in Science & Engineering**, 2(2), 1-14, February, www.ijarse.com, A. R. Research Publication, New Delhi

Yadav D. K. & **Sen** D. K. (2016), First Conjecture on Nonelementary Functions, http://www.grin.com/en/e-book/342263/first-conjecture-on-nonelementary-functions

Yadav D. K. & **Sen** D. K. **(2013)**, Proof of Second Standard Form of Nonelementary Functions, **I. J. of Advanced Research in Comp. Science & Soft. Engineering**, 3(2), 103-105, www.ijarcsse.com, Advance Research International Pub House, U. P.

Yadav D. K. & **Sen** D. K. **(2013)**, Proof of Third & Sixth Standard Forms of Nonelementary Functions, **Int. Journal of Advanced Research in Computer Science & Software Engineering**, 3(4), 247-257, www.ijarcsse.com, Advance Research Int. Publication House, U.P.

Yadav D. K. & **Sen** D. K. **(2013)**, Proof of Fourth Standard Form of Nonelementary Functions, **I. J. of Advanced Research in Comp. Science & Soft. Engineering**, 3(4), 258-264, www.ijarcsse.com, Advance Research International Pub House, U.P.

Yadav D. K. & **Sen** D. K. **(2013)**, Proof of Fifth Standard Form of Nonelementary Functions, **I. J. of Advanced Research in Comp. Science & Soft. Engineering**, 3(4), 269-274, www.ijarcsse.com, Advance Research International Pub House, U.P.

Yadav D. K. **(2015)**, Early Basic Foundations of Modern Integral Calculus, **Int. J. of Education and Science Research Review**, Vol. 2, Issue-2, pp. 37-44, April, E-**ISSN:** 2348-6457, www.ijesrr.org

Yadav D. K. **(2012)**, A Study of Indefinite Nonintegrable Functions, **Ph. D. Thesis**, Vinoba Bhave University, Hazaribag, Jharkhand, India

Yadav D. K. **(2016)**, A Study of Indefinite Nonintegrable Functions, *GRIN Verlag Publishing*, **Germany**, ISBN: 9783668312784, www.grin.com/ebook/341510, http://www.grin.com /en/e-book/341510/a-study-of-indefinite-nonintegrable-functions.

Suggestion Box

Suggestions will be welcomed through email id

mdrdkyadav@gmail.com